Double Envelopment

by

Gary Beck

PURPLE UNICORN MEDIA

Published by Purple Unicorn Media

Double Envelopment
by Gary Beck

Author: Gary Beck
Contact via the publisher: info@purpleunicornmedia.com

Cover image by Robin Stacey

ISBN 978-1-910718-58-2

Dedication

To Nathan, a young reader
who should always continue
reading.

Acknowledgments

Poems from Double Envelopment have appeared in:

11th Guntur International Poetry Fest-2019, A New Ulster, Active Muse, Bewildering Stories,, BlogNostics, Credo Espoir, Dissident Voice, Dreich Magazine (Hybrid Press), Highland Park Poetry (Muses Gallery), Indian Periodical, Journal of Expressive Writing, Miller's Pond Poetry Magazine (H&H Press), Nine Muses Poetry, Oddball Magazine, Poetry Leaves (Waterford Township Public Library), Poetry Life & Times, Pulsar Poetry, Raw Dog Press, Setu Magazine, Taj Mahal Review (Cyberwit Publishing), The Orchards Poetry Journal, The Seventh Quarry Poetry Magazine, The Stray Branch, WestWard Quarterly,Winamop Magazine, WineDrunk SideWalk, Ygdrasil Journal

Contents

Unfair

A child asked me:
"Why do some people have so much
and some so little?"
I searched for words of comfort,
but found none.
I considered explanations,
greed, capitalism,
inherited wealth,
but they wouldn't mean anything
to a child.
The best I could manage,
"It's always been that way,"
brought a cry of despair:
"It's not fair!"
In an anguished voice
at the shock of inequality,
in a woeful lament
that redress of grievances
would not be answered.

Urban Sight

The creaky, old homeless woman,
ravaged by unmet demands
pulls her cart of broken dreams
as she trudges unkind streets
that do not welcome outcasts,
concrete without compassion
for relics of once normal lives.

Immigrant

I carry the delivery bag
and no one looks at me.
They ignore the delivery boy
and I can't tell them
I'm a man, not a boy.
I hate my boss
who talks down to me,
because I'm an immigrant.
I hate the people who tip me
as much as those who don't.
They are all the same,
despising me.
I try not to think of the old days
when I walked with Shining Path,
carried an AK-47...
No one laughed at me then.
Now I am a delivery boy
and must eat my pride.

Removal

Winter winds blow harshly
on the abandoned homeless
marooned on city streets
'til rain and snow drive them off,
no choice but to leave behind
cardboard signs imploring aid,
cardboard mattresses, cardboard blankets
decomposing from the torrent
that washes away the last hope
for primitive survival
before eradication.

The Way

In the ongoing war
between capital and labor
that surely started in the caves
if not sooner,
labor almost always lost,
except for a brief time
in 1940s America,
when unions exerted
temporary strength
that compelled concurrence
from begrudging bosses.

Then capital developed
international mobility
and no longer needed
American workers
who gave their best
on the assembly lines,
but cost too much
and made too many demands
to be treated with care.

So the lords of profit
closed their factories,
abandoned the workers
who made them rich
and built in third world countries
where labor was cheap
and not empowered.

The decline of the blue collar class
eroded the foundation of the nation
built on sweat and muscle,
now replaced by hi-tech

service jobs for the underclass,
unadaptable
to the Information Age.

So the Land of Promise,
the hope of the mass of humanity,
now resembles other lands
where the rich rule,
their servants prosper
while the rest of us
struggle to survive.

Share and...

The great divide
between haves and have nots
is never wider
then at Christmas,
when the wealthy celebrate
on their super yachts
with epicurean pleasures,
while many huddle
in pubic housing
without heat, amenities,
each day a struggle
to endure poverty,
while only a few
can better the lives
of their disadvantaged children.

Lost

When a man lives on the street
he is a true citizen
of the disadvantaged world.
Nairobi, Calcutta, New York…
Did I say New York?
How can the richest city
ignore the abandoned
begging on street corners,
cardboard signs held low
the flags of disenfranchisement.
As the limousines drive by
the occupants do not notice
outcasts of despair.

What is Democracy?

Hundreds of thousands of homeless
trying to subsist on the streets?
Millions of children undernourished,
while the 1% feast?
Millions and millions of children
denied opportunity,
the system too poor to sustain them,
while it gives tax breaks to the rich?
A selfish ignoramus
wants to build a wall
between two friendly countries,
instead of rebuilding
the decaying infrastructure?
This is not what they taught
in grade schools around the land.
They tried to fill our heads
with ideal sentiments
based on noble documents
that promised… So so much.
And I was too young
to know the difference
between the word and the deed,
as teachers brainwashed us
to blindly accept
a nation that had nothing to do
with harsh reality.
And all the unanswered questions
why America the beautiful,
the land of plenty
didn't have enough for so many.
A beleaguered President once said:
'A house divided can not stand'.
Our divisions are as extreme
as that of the Bourbons and Romanoffs

from their oppressed people.
Is the hope of equality an illusion?
Is revolution the only way
to bring fairness to the people?

Climate Change

The sparrows sit in woeful rows
on trees beginning to bud
singing together sorrowfully,
'Where is Spring? Where is Spring?'
Most of us are shedding feathers.
Many are doing the mating dance.
Some are stealing twigs for our nests.
We're doing everything
that sparrows have always done
to continue bird existence,
but it hasn't gotten warmer
and if we don't huddle together
we won't survive the long, cold night.

What Creator is This?

The political scene
in America
has always delivered surprises,
men elected to the Presidency
who were inexperienced,
some of them unqualified,
but none compare to Trump,
totally unfit for high office.
Yet he appealed to enough voters
and with a great deal of help
from the Electoral College
managed to get elected
to the highest office in the land,
also becoming Commander-in-Chief
of a major nuclear power,
with absolutely no knowledge
of military affairs,
foreign affairs, economics,
except how to cheat others,
an inveterate liar
a mean and nasty bully,
with a lack of ethics and morals
that does not prevent
rabid supporters from admiring him,
a sad testament
to the quality of some citizens,
who probably never ask:
'Should Trump be a role model
for my children?'

Spectator

I sit in a building lobby
in midtown Manhattan
looking out the window
watching people flow by,
a continuous spectacle
of diverse humanity,
all races, all countries
represented in the city
of true internationalism.
Only the 1% don't appear,
mostly confining themselves
to luxury environments,
leaving average citizens,
the growing poverty class,
to share crumbing streets
with the abandoned homeless.

The Smell of the City

Modern cities are alike,
polluted air from fossil fuel,
insufficient greenery
for proper respiration,
poverty pockets of frustration
at rampant inequality
with distrust of prosperity.
The bang and boom of construction,
the homeless begging on the street,
people rushing, rushing, rushing
to work, school, shop, play,
all the urban functions
that mentor the cycle of extinction,
above all the stench of betrayal
of millions who left farms and towns
seeking a better life,
squandered in the indifferent city.

Alien Relations

We sent the equivalent
of the Nina, or Half Moon
out of our solar system,
Voyager I,
Voyager II,
announcing
our existence to the galaxy.
If there's alien life out there
and they're more advanced
and notice our primitive messengers
and decide to visit us,
is it reasonable to assume
they will come in peace?
After all
when did human explorers
ever come in peace?

Spam

One hundred years ago
a great war ended
that brought innovation
to the peace time world
that was never really peaceful,
but the massive upheaval
had exhausted so many
there was little concern
for small conflicts,
as 19th century minds
tried to catch up
to a frantic new pace
that animated life.

Deadly Greed

When I was young
I dreamed of a better world,
not without war, disease,
violent acts of nature,
but one without hunger,
where children were protected
and had a chance to grow
and use their best potential.
I tried my best
to make a difference
and helped some,
but not enough to change
the painful destiny
of so many,
defeated without a chance
by rampant inequality.

Shackles of Oppression

Capitalism has destroyed
the fabric of America,
offshoring, outsourcing,
reducing the unions
until they are too weak
to resist the oligarchs
who control almost everything,
leaving the rest of us in bondage.

The Lost

The mad walk city streets
mostly poor and desiccated,
raving and cursing wildly,
almost seeking to provoke
a violent response
to rabid outpourings
of irrationality,
attention-getting behavior
the last resort
of the mentally departed.

Lower Learning

When I was young
I didn't know enough about government
to have any idea how it worked,
who made it run.
Like many other youths
I accepted at face value
what they taught in school,
which made government seem
a lot better than school
with boring rote learning,
teacher oppression, bullying.
But as I got older
I began to discover
school was the training ground
for all the abusers
that plague our nation
and it may have been constricting,
but it wasn't chaotic
like the land I love.

Depletion Allowance

The Kennedy Administration
proudly proclaimed
the Peace Corps,
a democratic gift,
humanitarian aid
to needy countries
throughout the world,
and sent America's best,
not always the brightest,
but definitely the best
for selfless service.
And we the people applauded,
not realizing
we sere sending our best abroad
when they were needed at home.
But the lure of foreign travel
was far more romantic
than local residence
in an American backwater.

Dependency

The need to rely on others
is a serious burden
made heavier by obligations
to those being tended,
especially the mentally ill,
infirm, aged, no hope of cure,
just the daily effort
of service, care, attention,
a continuous demand
finally resolved
by emancipating death.

High Crimes

The officials,
elected and appointed,
who facilitated
the departure of American industry
betrayed the blue collar class,
a vital part of the nation,
jobs lost in the homeland
that once supported millions
now safely eviscerated,
leaving the unions impotent
no longer able
to resist the oligarchs.

Endemic Decay

One month before Spring
and many New Yorkers
are putting away coats
anticipating warmth,
not understanding
that climate change
alters the weather pattern
and we no longer have
well-defined seasons,
little snow in winter,
few hot days in summer,
nature in revolt
against years of abuse.

Prisoner of Progress

Once I did not know the internet,
Amazon, Facebook, Goodreads,
and I didn't have email,
just the U.S. Mail,
bills, rent, advertisements,
it took a little while to get there.
Now I use my tablet for everything,
engaged electronically.
When my email was locked up
so was my digital life.
I'm so accustomed to hi-tech
that I can't go back to analog.

On Inequality

Celebrities are arrested
for bribing to get their children
into a prestigious college,
while indentured legislators
gave away a trillion dollars
to corporations and the rich,
a massive embezzlement
of funds vitally needed
for our collapsing infrastructure.
Yet these capitol thieves
suffered no consequences
for looting the public treasury,
as obsessed parents,
objects of the public scorn
will soon be convicted
of high crimes and misdemeanors.

Liberty in Ashes

So many want to be president.
So few know that it should be
the protector of the people,
guarding them from oppression.
Instead, these wannabe servants
eager for indenture
to the capitalist masters
who have established control
of the future of America
having successfully removed
the stout-hearted blue collar class,
the only group determined enough
to resist the blatant tyranny
of voracious oligarchs,
refusing to give a fair share
to the people who toil for them
while they consume the fruits of the earth.

Growth Spurt

The march of civilization
has improved life for many,
who live longer, healthier,
with luxuries unimagined
a few hundred years ago.
As we evolved
from family, to clan, to tribe,
then made the great leap
to nation states
we devoured the resources
of a bountiful earth,
until we are poised
to destroy the world
in extravagant consumption.

High Crime II

The prison industry,
the most unproductive industry
in this ailing nation
currently incarcerates
more than a million men,
a lot of women,
more then the population
of some small countries.
The system employs
guards, cooks, teachers,
psychologists, doctors,
the list goes on,
all to maintain
adjudicated criminals,
innocent or guilty,
custodians or confined
another pustulant body
in diseased America.

Similar or ...

New Year's Eve 1968,
a terrible year for Vietnamese,
while only some Americans
lost loved ones,
as the nation consumed
vast amounts of treasure
that the oligarchs believed
would be wasted on the people.
Despite growing inequality
most of us didn't notice,
unless our sons were killed
in distant jungles.
We still didn't realize
that the lords of profit
were abandoning our factories,
eliminating blue collar workers,
the last group to defy the bosses.
Yet I seem to remember
it was a good year for Haut Brion.

New Year's Eve 2018,
the revelers no longer hulk
in one congested mass
jammed crammed together,
thousands drunk, stoned,
muggers, pickpockets, hoodlums
visiting their neighbors,
who still had a great time.
Now people stand
in isolated groups,
regimented in the Age of Terror.
But despite the lack of drink, drugs,
they still have a good time.

Visual

Visual images
on electronic screens
tantalize
young viewers
who do not understand
why they cannot have
the same things
as everyone else,
poverty parents
never able
to satisfactorily explain
inequality.

Emergency Alert

As America subsides
into increasing poverty,
incrementing apathy
for those who cannot profit
from an unfair system
favoring the rich
grown so powerful
they're no longer concerned
with the well-being of the people
who still do the tasks
that keep society running.
There is a great danger
that unless we arrest
the slide to decline
clinical despair
will permeate the land,
accelerating dissolution.

Beset

A semblance of normality
pervades the land,
even for the disadvantaged
struggling as usual
to make ends meet,
feed, shelter, clothe
their needy children,
who will never understand
why they can't have
the same things
as everyone else.

Fleeting Ideals

I sometimes wonder
if the brilliant men
who once conceived
of life, liberty and the pursuit…
really believed what they wrote,
or were already an integral part
of the ruling class,
replacing kings
with oligarchs,
even more ruthless
than sovereigns,
who sometimes considered
the good of the realm.
The new masters
conquering the world
with wealth, not arms,
only fighting for nationalism,
economic exploitation,
changing existence
for oppressed people
seeing the light dim
in submerging America.

Non-Emergency Visit

The wait at the doctor's office
gets longer and longer.
Aching, frightened patients sit,
some stand it is so crowded.
The clerks sit at their desks
hiding behind computers,
begrudgingly acknowledge a patient,
begrudge any information,
begrudge common courtesy,
let along compassion
for ailing visitors.

Retooling

For hundreds of years
men developed skills in chess
improving the level of play.
Then a computer beat the world champion,
outcalculating him,
but not many realized
men programmed the machine.
Now the newest computer,
virtually A.I.,
outthinks the world champions
and can do it in Go, checkers,
even monopoly,
replacing men's minds
with advanced software.

Limitations

A new year
in besieged America,
enemies without and within
conflicting
on a tiny planet
with brutal indifference
for varied life forms
struggling for survival
in deadly competition,
while only humans
have the capacity
to preserve existence,
instead squandering the future
in meaningless squabbles.

Civilization

The changing of the seasons
when people lived on farms
meant traditional rituals
for planting, harvesting,
other activities
regulated by nature,
early to bed,
early to rise,
didn't make us wise,
but had a reassuring order,
except when disaster struck,
then the struggle to endure
dominated the days.
City dwellers
have forgotten
the schedule of nature,
except to put on
or take off
light or heavy clothing,
waking for work, school,
not tending the fields
no longer competent
in the production of crops.

Abrasion

The dignity of man
is maintained
by courtesy, respect
and lots of patience
with the foibles of others.
Those of us
who are incapable
of good behavior,
the social contract
to get along with others,
go through conflict
clashing with the hostile
on every level,
mental, emotional, physical,
until small confrontations
become large conflagrations.

Harsh Winter

The colder it gets
the more clothes people wear,
except the abandoned homeless
shivering on street corners,
the human refuse of capitalism
rejected from society,
little to no concern
why these outcasts
no longer of redeeming value,
treated slightly better than lepers,
no interest in learning why
they were subtracted from care.

Late

The alarm clock didn't go off,
so I overslept.
Anne didn't get up,
so I missed breakfast.
The garage door got stuck again,
then the car wouldn't start.
I cursed it, but that didn't help.
I rushed to Grove Street
and just missed the commuter bus.
Dave from Agriculture stopped for me,
otherwise I would have missed half a day.
He dropped me off at Commerce,
I rushed in ready to kill
for a cup of coffee,
then Stanly, the snotty supervisor,
told me Trump shut down the government,
so we've all been furloughed.
Now what do I do
without a salary?

Scientific Advances

The world has always verged
on devouring chaos,
but not until the Atomic Age
did mankind have the power
to terminate existence.
Meteor strike, earthquake,
forces of nature
didn't destroy all life.
Now, courtesy of science,
there is ample means
nuclear, chemical, biological,
to eradicate animals, vegetables,
until all we're left with
is a lunar landscape.

Je Rends Grace

I give thanks each day
that I am still here,
allowed to enjoy
breathable air,
able to look at
wonders of man and nature,
fortunate to forget
for a brief interlude
the evil we do
that makes life worse.

Class Warfare

A President, ideally,
should lead the nation
in dignity, with respect
for all citizens, charged
by the Constitution
to serve and protect
regardless of differences.
Our current elected leader,
like many elected officials
has forgotten, or never knew
the duty owed to America.
Instead of reaching out to all
he erodes the middle class,
deaccesses the working class,
neglects the poverty class,
until we are divided
so the servants of the oligarchs
can easily conquer us.

High Crimes III

American politics
are crazier
then other countries' politics.
We may not have overt coups,
but the oligarchs ensure
no one can alter
established privileges,
though they endanger
the eroding environment,
the declining middle class,
the growing poverty class,
allowing a national debt
that will asphyxiate our future,
as long as the rich have comforts
denied so many others.

A Dimming Light

I walk the crumbling streets
of a city in turmoil,
citizens rioting,
services disrupted,
violent clashes
between hostile groups
leave dead and wounded,
then the shock to the senses,
it's not a third world country
but the good old U.S.A.,
quick to proclaim democracy,
slow to live up to it.

Parable

The sparrows were fighting this morning
over mating, nesting, territory
because they think it's Spring.
Instincts of these urgent creatures
to battle to continue the species,
comforts and security secondary,
unlike ravenous mankind,
some of us so greedy
we will do anything for gain,
whether at the expense of others,
or destroying the weak and helpless.
The birds, despite their ferocity,
do limited harm,
while the intelligent species
ravage the earth.

Political Season

The presidential candidates
come out of the woodwork like bugs
to feast on the diseased body
of decaying America,
each one less qualified than the other,
all proclaiming their abilities,
all looking sincere and caring,
all hired by the oligarchs
to serve the needs of the wealthy,
while trying to convince the people
the needs of the nation come first.

Ode to the Brave

The bravest people
in New York City
are the blind,
who traverse difficult streets
only using a cane,
travel hard enough
for the unimpaired,
let alone those who cannot see
hidden obstacles.

That Time of Year

Spring traditionally meant
the planting of crops,
invasions first by tribes,
then by armies
taking advantage
of fair weather
for normal activity,
growth and destruction.
Advanced technology
allows year round planting, war,
no longer dependent
on benevolent climate,
energies misdirected
to erosive outcomes.

Cities

People walk unheeding streets
that do not care if rich or poor,
made with low bid concrete
that will not outlast the pyramids,
but should be appreciated
for ephemeral engineering.

Appointment

The waiting room is crowded.
The patients sit packed together,
yet isolated in their fear.
The doctors walk by
always looking busy,
always looking serious,
which makes people nervous
as they await their turn
for treatment, good or bad news,
whatever is scheduled
on the medical menu,
the visit a necessity,
regardless of apprehensions,
not a recreational moment.

Dabbler

A Presidential phenomenon
that only a year at the job
ages the incumbent noticeably,
except for the current occupant
not affected like others,
because of lack of involvement,
not knowing responsibilities,
what he should do for the nation,
a slightly bloated plutocrat
who represents the worst
of the failures of democracy.

Park Life

Tourists and locals enjoy the day.
Daffodils are blooming.
The carousel is packed with kids.
The birds are chirping: 'Spring. Spring.'
Some people are wearing t-shirts.
No one notices the homeless
in their own temporary cocoon
oblivious to joy of the day,
eroded by the struggle
that goes on continually,
a testament to human spirit
that despite deprivation
they will not lie down and die.

Genetic Benefit

People walk the streets
going about their business
completely unaware
that disaster can strike
at almost any moment
injuring or ending lives.
Yet the hardy human race
is characterized
by the will to survive
regardless of suffering,
the best quality
of a contentious species.

Betrayed

The more I look at people
in my divided land
the unhappier they seem,
faces mostly fixed in frowns,
lips pressed tight together,
portraits of disappointment
at unfulfilled desires,
bitter failure at shattered hopes,
the last vestiges of expectation
methodically eradicated.

Ah, Technology

Survival challenged minds
blindly walk city streets
completely absorbed
in hand-held devices,
texting obliviously
to possible hazards,
obstacles in the path,
bumping into passersby,
totally unaware
of the dangers they face
by not paying attention
to where they're walking.

Historical Farewells

Sometimes it's difficult
to understand how everyone felt
when a civilization collapsed.
It took Rome hundreds of years
for its great expansion to crumble.
The British empire dissolved
from the burden of two World Wars.
The brief American Empire
barely lasted fifty years.
Then imperial overreach,
diminutive leaders
combined to eliminate
the illusion of power
consigning its people
to poverty.

Evil Deeds

A blinding fog of ignorance
only surpassed by endless greed
continues to pollute the land,
a few manipulating many
to desire and acquire more,
never allowing satiation,
continuously offering
the newest, best technology,
an insidious diversion,
while those who never get enough,
thwarted by insufficient means,
festering with frustration,
victimize the innocent
when they can't get the latest phone.

Blind to Emergencies

Only forty or fifty years ago
we had regular seasons.
Spring would turn warm
when it was supposed to.
The other seasons
changed as expected
as we went through activities
predictably scheduled.
Then climate change began,
weather pattern unstable,
with uncertain conditions,
too little snow,
not enough hot days,
fierce storms, wild fires,
while the leaders of the land
refused to take action
to save the planet.

Cure Needed

Our land of insane violence
is perilously diseased
with the need to hurt others,
spreading more and more brutally,
warped minds inventing new ways
to inflict lurid suffering,
while our confused society
accepts harmful afflictions,
disturbingly, as if normal,
many of us oblivious
to the dangers of contagion.

Flash Glance

The wisteria are blooming
on a tired old vine
attached to a tired old house.
The vine has not been tended
and the blossoms are sparse,
yet on close inspection
they're delicately beautiful.
So few of the passersby
notice nature's brief treat,
fragile petals for a moment,
then gone, as fleeting as life.

What Have We Become?

We have moved into a stasis,
the era of the unqualified.
President Obama became
the least experienced POTUS,
but actually did a fair job.
Then Trump was elected,
the most unqualified ever,
setting a precedent
for anyone to be President.

Waste

A beautiful spring day.
In an idyllic world
we would all pursue
peaceful pleasures.
But global greed,
lust for power
corrupts our better nature,
driving us to evil deeds,
committing every kind of crime,
every kind of perversion,
inevitably destroying
ourselves, our planet.

Same, same

Locals come to Bryant Park
on weekends crowded with tourists,
but they're not much different,
all brought up with tv, the internet,
most with sufficient protein
to be about the same height,
similar clothing,
only language sets them apart,
but not too much,
urban life homogenizing
making aliens akin.

Varicose Impatience

It took a long time
for horse-pulled wagons
to be replaced
by motorized buses.
The elderly and infirm
who never would have stood
while the horses were trotting
now rush to the door
with cane or crutches
before the bus stops,
unable to wait
to be the first one off.

Holiday Time, New York City

Schools are closed
and lots of young people
come to the skating rink
at Bryant Park.
The ice is crowded,
but most of the skaters
are enjoying themselves.
A few struggle,
mastery of the blades
eluding them.
A few lack the will
to persevere
after repeated falls.
Most realize
they must keep trying
if they want to skate.

Giving

Christmas is coming,
just a few weeks away
and many are buying online,
or rushing to stores
shopping for presents
conditioned by generations of tv
to spend, spend, spend,
confused about
the nature of giving,
money became the measurement,
creating envy in the poor
who can't afford extravagant gifts
their children see going to others.

Oversights

A great flaw
in the Constitution
of the United States of…
is that it lacks an amendment
allowing intelligence tests
for Presidential candidates.
An even greater neglect
is the lack of sanity tests
for the elected President.

Perspective

The policies of a country
are much more consequential
then the problems
of individuals,
but when people experience
the pains and pleasure
of their normal lives
they always seem more important
then the fate of the nation.

Enemy of the People

We elect a President
to serve the nation,
care for our citizens,
even those who didn't vote for him.
It sometimes takes a while
to discover the hard way
we selected the wrong man.
This time many of us knew
he was completely unfit,
but it was a fait accompli
with no recourse.
Yet embittered voters
cursed and reviled him,
not realizing
this strengthened his supporters,
who apparently didn't care
Trump was a negative role model
for their children.
His decisions became questionable,
irresponsible,
downright dangerous.
Then he shut down the government,
making some of us wonder
if he was a lunatic,
a monster, or both.

Military Quandary

If Generals and Admirals
know machines can outthink them
will they listen to advice
in war-gaming scenarios
to attack first,
or suffer a devastating first strike?

Eternal Question

The day before Christmas
and all through the world
distraction torments the people,
even those with Christian spirit.
War, famine, disease, flood,
the list of disasters goes on and on…
Death does not recognize
the annual holiday
dispensing the usual despair,
so many suffering
while others feast,
impossible to comprehend
the unfairness of life.

Breakdown

The President should be
caretaker of the government,
protector of the people,
yet he shuts it down
depriving many of salaries
that also affects farmers, businesses,
possibly the economy.
Now he wants to take the money
meant for disaster relief
for Puerto Rico, Florida,
even California,
blaming the state for the wildfires
due to bad forest management.
He's ready to destroy the country
to build a wall between friends,
policies so irrational
they endanger the future of the nation.

The More Deceived

The morning birds chirped of Spring
deceived by treacherous Groundhogs
who may have seen their shadows,
but are ignorant of climate change,
snug in their glass enclosures
treated more like pets then low beasts
at least once a year on G Day.
So a few warm days fool people,
some putting away their sweaters.
When winter storms surprise the city
some of us may remember
we were duped by rodents.

Want Not

As Christmas draws near
the wealthy are relaxed.
They can afford
expensive gifts
that will delight all.
The poor are stressed,
unable to purchase
the tantalizing goods
their children see
every day on tv,
who cannot understand
why they cannot have
what other kids have.

Fleeting Splendor

Spring is just around the corner
and trees are beginning to bud,
except the fragile cherry trees
that will have a brief explosion
of delirious color and smell,
then the frail blossoms will fall
and the lush green leaves
will look like any other tree.

What Profiteth...

In a shameful episode
in American history
Trump was elected President.
After making a mess
of almost everything
foreign and domestic,
he's running for re-election,
no surprise knowing who he is,
the real shock, his supporters,
still fervently loyal
despite his lies and abuses,
making me question
voter's sanity or intelligence.

It's Still Cold Out

Spring is almost sprung
and I know where the boidies is,
but the grass ain't riz,
it's cold as heck,
man and beast are complaining,
when will it get warm?

Prognostication

A winter freeze set in
across much of the country
called a polar vortex.
People are dressed for the cold
wearing multiple layers
and everyone's complaining
it's never been like this before.
Then surprise. It's Groundhog Day!
Chuck and Phil do their stuff,
come out of the rodent den,
don't see their shadows,
don't get a chance to bite anyone,
back they go and some fools believe
they predicted early spring,
quickly forgotten if they're wrong.

Nice Day

It actually feels like spring today.
The sun is shining, there's no wind.
It's supposed to go up to 67F.
But I'm still wearing my warm coat,
because ever since they got PhD's
I don't trust meteorologists,
who aren't as accurate
as the Farmer's Almanac.
So I try to appreciate
every day, regardless of weather,
for my time is running short
and I need to enjoy
whatever I have left.

High Office

I think about our President
who I consider a disgrace
in our atrophied democracy,
it is hard to imagine
this braggart, liar, bully
enjoying nature's wonders,
a Robin saying: 'Spring. Spring.'
cherry trees in exquisite blossom.
I pity the poverty president
blind to the wonder of life,
immersed in selfish ego trips,
polluting the land with his greed,
oblivious to the needs of the people.

Coming Soon

A warm day in early February,
everyone believed the Groundhogs
who didn't see their shadows
and think Spring is near.
They'll learn the hard way
not to trust rodents
when the next snowstorm
paralyzes the city.

The Band is Playing

A parade in New York City.
Sikhs? Swedes? No. Scots.
I can tell by the kilts and bagpipes.
They gather in Bryant Park,
practice on the drums,
warm up the pipes,
a lively, trilling sound
competing with sirens
enriching the city.
Tourists stop to camera
another sight to show back home,
photographic proof
that New York City
is the ethnic capitol
of the world.

The Justice System

An obscure lawyer
sued a sleazy President
in a sleazy lawsuit
that distracted the public
from greater crimes
that did long term harm
to a vulnerable nation.
But the President escaped
from legal consequences
and continues to afflict the land,
dividing his time between golf
and ways to harm America.
While the obscure lawyer
who challenged an immoral man
is now under assault
accused of many crimes,
ending his threat to the ego-in-chief.

Watch the Birdy

The day after spring
I saw a young Robin,
a perky handsome lad
who didn't want to be looked at.
I love to watch birds
so I looked at him,
which he didn't appreciate,
giving me angry glances.
I didn't want to upset him
but my need to see him
intruded on his privacy
and he flew off,
squawking bird imprecations
for the interruption.

The Evolution of Chess

A strong computer
beat the World Champion human.
A stronger computer
beat the strong one.
A smarter computer
beat the stronger one,
permanently ending
dominance of grandmasters,
who will be eclipsed
in human/A.I. tournaments.

Psychological Gleanings

A group of psychiatrists
made a study of the dangers
a lunatic president
could cause the government.
They identified
disruptions to the economy,
assaults on the environment,
consorting with our enemies,
betraying our allies,
deceiving the people,
concealing his crimes,
attacking anyone
who disagrees with him.
Once they analyzed the data
they were shocked to discover
they had profiled President Trump.

Rain Day

A rainy day in the park,
but it's spring,
so tourists are clicking away
with phone cameras,
without stopping to look,
urgent to record
for the folks back home,
who would enjoy the trip second hand
almost as much as the travelers.

Storm Warning

A winter storm is coming,
the first of the season.
New York City gets tense.
The Mayor orders
emergency preparations,
having learned, like all politicians,
that discomfort for the public
costs votes at election time.
We may question if they care
but they're doing their job
protecting citizens,
not as hardy as their forebears,
no longer able to withstand
a little bit of snow,
a little bit of ice.

Easement

Now that Spring is here
people are kinder,
more relaxed,
stress shed
along with excess clothes.
problems may still be severe,
but easier to endure
without the burden
of heavy coats.

Musing

The cherry blossoms have fallen,
brief beauty gone.
Will we bloom again?

Gary Beck

Gary Beck has spent most of his adult life as a theater director. He has 14 published chapbooks. His poetry collections include: *Days of Destruction* (Skive Press), *Expectations* (Rogue Scholars Press). *Dawn in Cities, Assault on Nature, Songs of a Clerk, Civilized Ways, Displays, Perceptions, Fault Lines, Tremors, Perturbations, Rude Awakenings, The Remission of Order* and *Contusions* (Winter Goose Publishing). *Desperate Seeker* will be published by Winter Goose Publishing. *Conditioned Response* (Nazar Look). *Resonance* (Dreaming Big Publications). *Virtual Living* (Thurston Howl Publications). *Blossoms of Decay, Expectations, Blunt Force* and *Transitions (*Wordcatcher Publishing). *Temporal Dreams* and *Mortal Coil* will be published by Wordcatcher Publishing. His novels include: *Extreme Change* (Cogwheel Press), *Flawed Connections* (Black Rose Writing), *Call to Valor* and *Crumbling Ramparts* (Gnome on Pigs Productions). As part of the continuing series, '*Stand to Arms Marines*', Gnome on Pigs Productions will publish the third book in the series, *Raise High the Walls. Sudden Conflicts* (Lillicat Publishers). *Acts of Defiance* and *Flare Up* (Wordcatcher Publishing). S*till Defiant* (The sequel to *Acts of Defiance*) will be published by Wordcatcher Publishing. *Extreme Change* will be published by Winter Goose Publishing. His short story collections include, *A Glimpse of Youth* (Sweatshoppe Publications). *Now I Accuse and other stories (*Winter Goose Publishing). *Dogs Don't Send Flowers and other stories* (Wordcatcher Publishing). *The Republic of Dreams and other essays* (Gnome on Pig Productions). *The Big Match and other one act plays* will be published by Wordcatcher Publishing. His original plays and translations of Moliere, Aristophanes and Sophocles have been produced Off Broadway. His poetry, fiction and essays have appeared in hundreds of literary magazines. He lives in New York City.

Printed in Great Britain
by Amazon